ASSESSING YOUR CHILD'S PROGRESS

Testing and assessment in the National Curriculum

Pupils between the ages of 7 and 11 (Years 3–6) cover Key Stage 2 of the National Curriculum. In May of their final year of Key Stage 2 (Year 6) all pupils take written National Tests (commonly known as SATs) in the three most important subjects: English, Mathematics and Science. Your child may already have taken some National Tests at the end of Key Stage 1 (Year 2). These will have been in number, shape and space, reading, writing, handwriting and spelling.

At the end of Key Stage 1, your child will have been awarded a National Curriculum level for each subject tested. When your child eventually takes the Key Stage 2 tests, he or she again will be awarded a level. On average, pupils are expected to advance one level for every two years they are at school. The target for pupils at the end of Key Stage 1 is Level 2. By the end of Key Stage 2, four years later, the target is Level 4. The table below will show you how your child should progress.

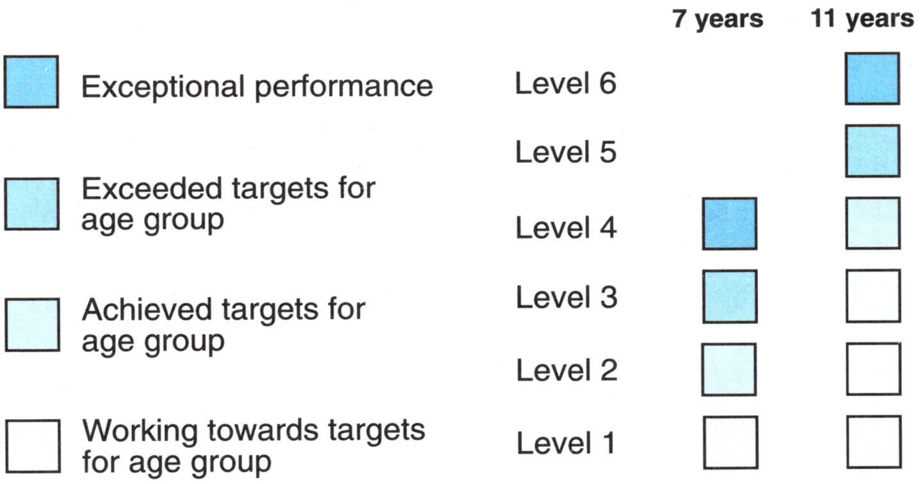

Assessing your child's progress throughout Key Stage 2 of the National Curriculum

The aim of the Letts Assessment books is to help you monitor your child's progress in English, Mathematics and Science throughout Key Stage 2. There are four books for each subject – one for each year, starting with 7–8 year olds. The questions in the books become progressively harder with each year, so that for 10–11 year olds, the questions will be at a level similar to the Key Stage 2 National Tests.

After completing a book, your child will have a score which you will be able to interpret using the progress indicator provided. This will give you a guide to the level at which your child is working.

ASSESSING YOUR CHILD'S PROGRESS

Using this book to assess your child's progress in Science

This book is for 9–10 year olds (Year 5). It contains four basic features:

Questions:	30 questions, arranged in order of difficulty as follows: 4 at Level 2 (pages 1–3) 9 at Level 3 (pages 4–13) 11 at Level 4 (pages 14–27) 6 at Level 5 (pages 28–35)
Answers:	showing acceptable responses and marks
Note to Parent:	giving advice on what your child should be doing and how to help
Progress Chart:	showing you how to interpret your child's marks to arrive at a level

- Your child should not attempt to do all the questions in the book in one go. Try setting ten questions at a time. If your child does not understand a question, you might want to explain it. Although the questions in this book are not meant to constitute a formal test, you should encourage your child to answer as many as possible without help. Read the questions to your child if you think it will help.
- When your child has completed the questions, turn to the Answer section at the back of the book. Using the recommended answers, award your child the appropriate mark or marks for each question. In the margin of each question page, there are small boxes. These are divided in half with the marks available for that question at the bottom, and a blank at the top for you to fill in your child's score.
- Collate your child's marks on the grid on page 46. Then add them up. Once you have the total, turn to page 36 at the front of the Answer section and look at the Progress Chart to determine your child's level.
- Work through the answers with your child, using the Note to Parent to help give advice, correct mistakes and explain problems.

Equipment your child will need for this book

All your child needs are a pen or pencil for writing, and a pencil for drawing. Your child may also like to have a rubber for changing answers. Where lines have to be drawn, they can be drawn either with a ruler or freehand, whichever your child feels most comfortable with.

LEVEL 2

MARKS

1 Here are some pictures of animals.

a Write the name of each animal in the correct circle.

4
Q1a

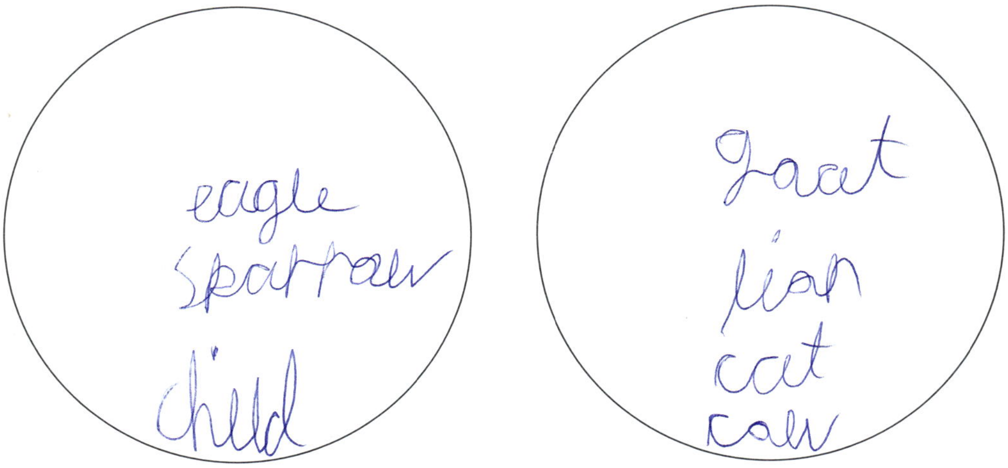

two-legged animals

four-legged animals

b How many of the two-legged animals have wings?

1
Q1b

2 ....

2 Below is a list of what some materials are used for.

Link each material with the reason it is used. The first one has been done for you.

Material	Reason
Ice is used in drinks because it is	soft
Iron is used for nails because it is	cold
Glass is used for windows because it is	hard
Foam is used in cushions because it is	see-through

3
Q2

3 Natalie has a rubber-band powered aircraft.

When she pulls the aircraft back, the rubber band changes.

Tick ✓ **two** changes that happen to the rubber band.

It gets fatter. ☐

It gets longer. ☑

It gets shorter. ☐

It gets thinner. ☑

2
Q3

4 When you let go of some objects they fall down **quickly**. Other objects fall down **slowly**.

a Tick ✓ **one** box for each object shown. The first one has been done for you.

Object	Falls quickly	Falls slowly
Paper aeroplane		✓
Pound coin	✓	
Feather		✓
Lump of plasticine	✓	✗
Air-filled balloon		✓

4
Q4a

b How could you make the paper aeroplane fall quickly?

by flicking it.

1
Q4b

5 Look at this picture of a pond.

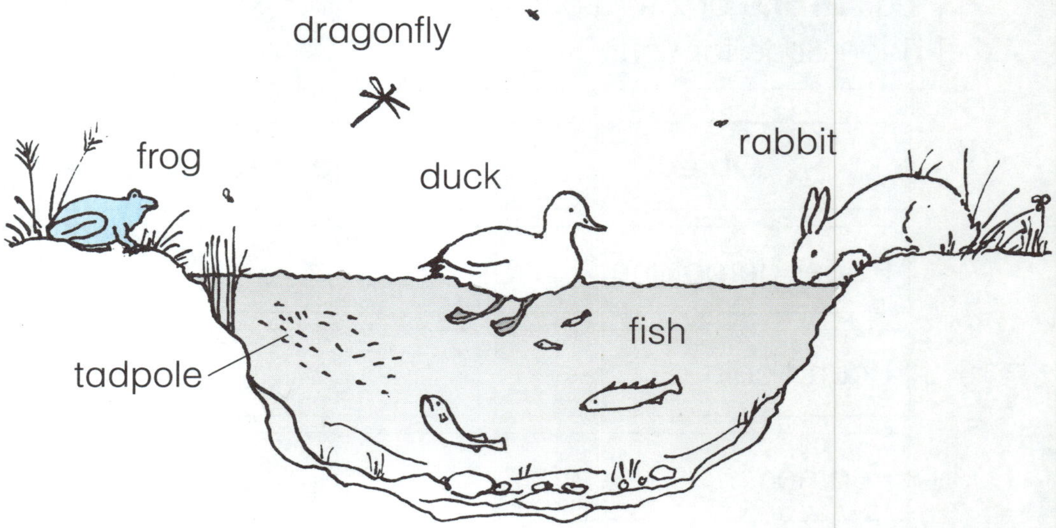

a Write down the names of the animals that live in the water all the time.

1 Q5a

fish X

b Write down the names of the animals that can fly.

1 Q5b

dragon fly

c What do these animals both have to help them fly?

1 Q5c

wings

Letts

MARKS

6 The picture shows part of a house being built.

Which of the materials are natural and which have to be made? Tick ✓ **one** box for each material.

	Natural	Made
Sand	☐	☐
Cement	☐	☐
Wood	☐	☐
Brick	☐	✓
Glass	☐	✓
Slate	☐	☐
Plastic	☐	☐

7
Q6

7 All of these things use electricity.

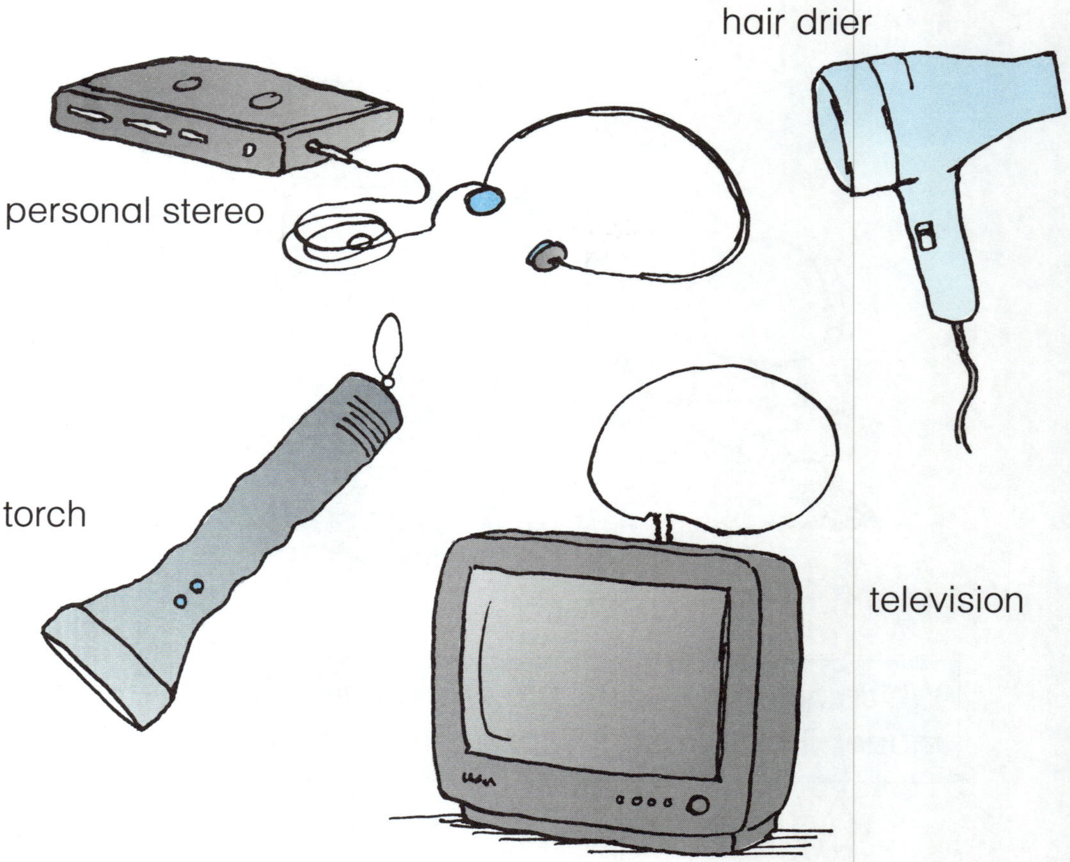

a Which one **only** gives out light?

~~telewition~~ tarch

1 Q7a

b Which one **only** gives out sound?

tv

1 Q7b

c Which one gives out light **and** sound?

tv

1 Q7c

MARKS

8 You have three different sorts of teeth.

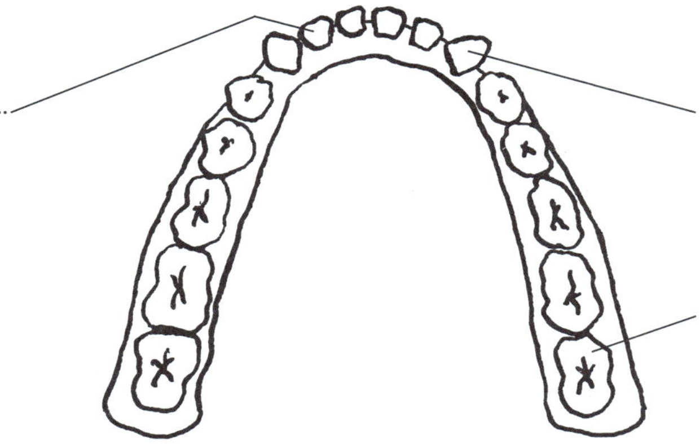

Incisors are for biting and cutting food.

Canines are for tearing food.

Molars are for chewing food.

a Label the teeth on the diagram.

3 Q8a

b Use words from the list to complete the sentences.

4 Q8b

decay	**toothbrush**	**two**	**dentist**	**meals**
toothpaste	**doctor**	**shower**	**soap**	**ten**

1 To clean your teeth you need a balhbrush ....
and some balhpaste paste ....

2 You should clean your teeth at least ..2.............. times a day after meals ....

3 To have your teeth checked, you should visit a dentist .... regularly.

4 If you do not clean your teeth properly they may decay ....

9 Materials can be changed in many different ways.

a What would happen to a spoonful of salt if you stirred it into a dish of water?

It would ~~go~~ be ~~saggy~~ crunchy.

1 Q9a

b What would happen to the water if you left it for a few weeks?

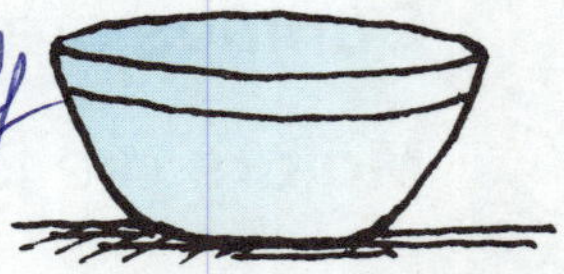

It would go saggy

1 Q9b

In some places, people have to boil the water to make it fit to drink.

c How can they cool the water down to make a cool drink?

1 Q9c

Darren's ice-pop has melted on his way home from school.

d What would happen to the ice-pop if he put it in the freezer?

It wouldn't melt.

1 Q9d

LEVEL 3

MARKS

e Dad has left the kettle boiling and the spout is near the window.

What would you see if you looked closely at the window?

yoll wolld See ?

1 Q9e

10 Look at these pictures of different materials.

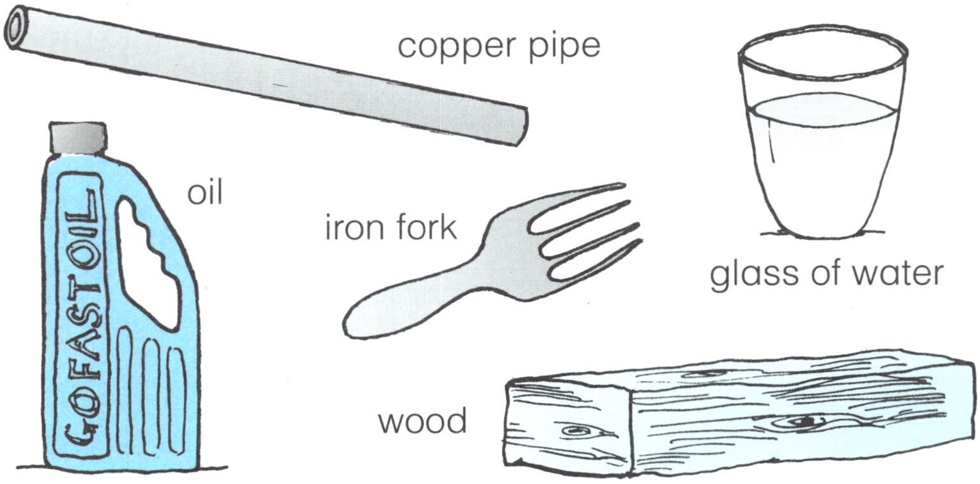

a Which **two** are liquids?

2 Q10a

b Which **two** are metals?

2 Q10b

c Which **one** could be burned on an open fire?

1 Q10c

11 This toy car is rolled down three different surfaces.

1 Q11a

a On which surface would the car travel slowest?

....

In an experiment, marbles are used as weights to make the car move on different surfaces.

Here are the results.

Surface	Number of marbles needed to move the car
Table top	5
Wallpaper	8
Sandpaper	10
Carpet	?

MARKS

b Underline the correct words in the brackets to complete the sentence.

1 Q11b

The car would need (more than/less than) 10 marbles to make it move on the carpet.

If a marble is dropped from a height of 10 metres it will travel to the ground quite quickly. You can slow it down with a parachute.

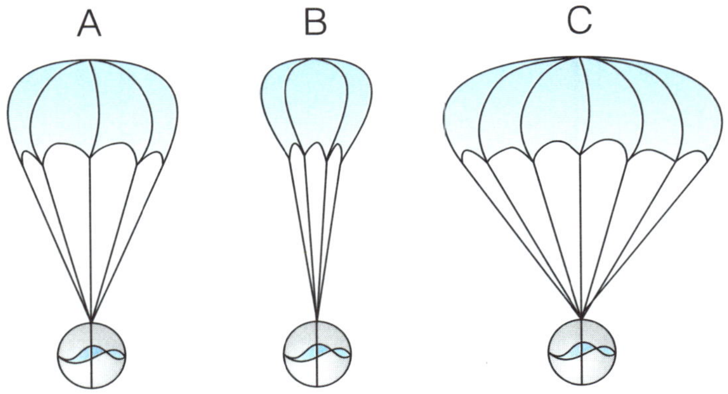

c Which marble, **A**, **B**, **C** or **D**, would have the slowest speed?

1 Q11c

Marble ....

d Why does this marble have the slowest speed?

1 Q11d

....

....

12

When the gun fires, there is a loud bang and smoke comes out.

a What would the soldier on Mount Vernon notice first, the smoke or the bang?

1 Q12a

....

Eddie is playing golf with his friend Ben.

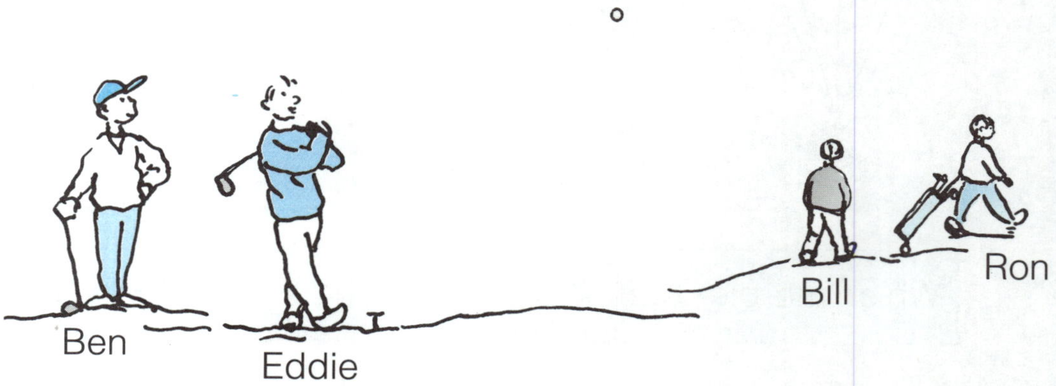

Eddie shouts "Fore" because he doesn't want the ball to hit his friends, Bill and Ron.

b Who would hear the shout loudest, Ben, Bill or Ron?

1 Q12b

....

c Why would he hear the shout louder than the others hear it?

1 Q12c

....

....

MARKS

13 Look at this bar chart. It shows how many children in a class wear each size of shoe.

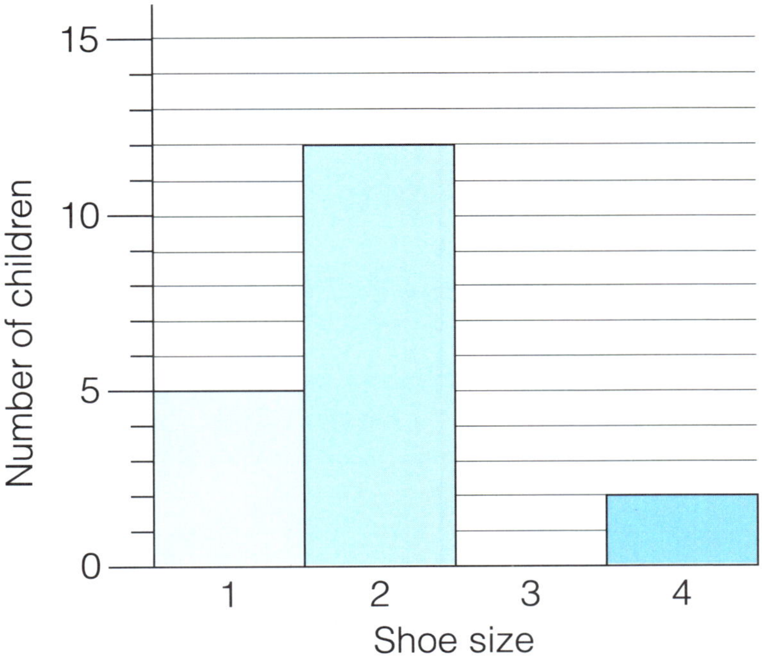

a Eight children wear size three shoes. Draw this as a bar on the chart.

1 Q13a

b Which size is worn by the most children?

....

1 Q13b

c How many children wear size four shoes?

....

1 Q13c

d How many children are there in the class?

....

1 Q13d

14 Some objects are attracted to magnets.

This magnet has picked up some drinks cans and left some behind.

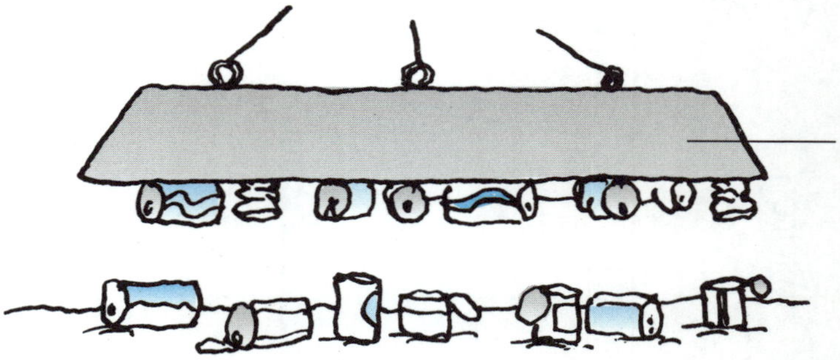

a What metal could the cans on the magnet be made of?

1 Q14a

....

Each of these magnets has a north and a south pole.

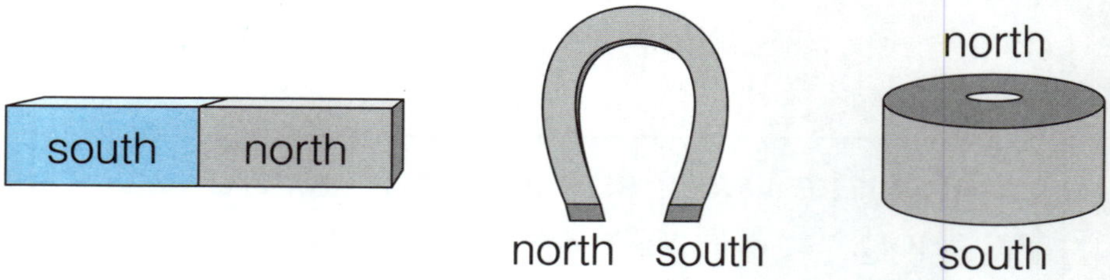

Look at the chart below.

	North pole of magnet	South pole of magnet
Steel can	attracts	attracts
South pole of magnet	attracts	repels
Steel comb	attracts	attracts
North pole of magnet	repels	attracts

MARKS

b Fill in the missing words from these sentences.

Opposite poles .... each other.

Like poles .... each other.

2 Q14b

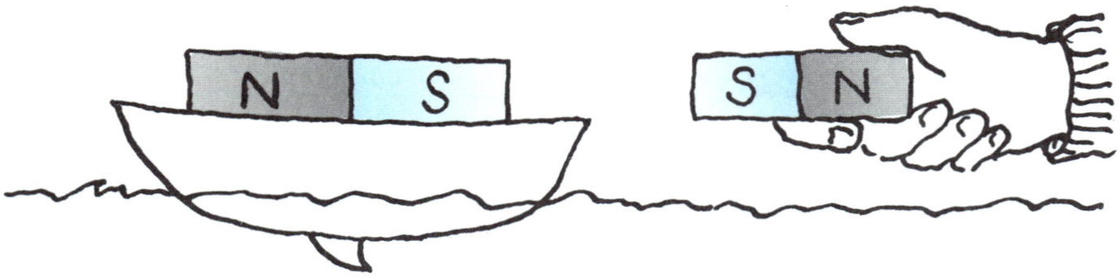

c What happens to the boat in this picture above?

....

1 Q14c

15 Look at this picture of Emma skateboarding.

a Draw an arrow on the picture to show which direction the skateboard will go.

1 Q15a

b Emma's shoe grips onto the ground. What is the force between the shoe and the ground called?

1 Q15b

....

16 As Jane walked around the garden she saw some animals. She used a key to find out what they were.

Has the animal got wings?

- yes → Are the wings brightly coloured?
  - yes → It is a **butterfly**.
  - no → It is a **wasp**.
- no → Does it have a shell?
  - yes → It is a **snail**.
  - no → It is a **caterpillar**.

a Use the key to write the correct name under each animal.

4 Q16a

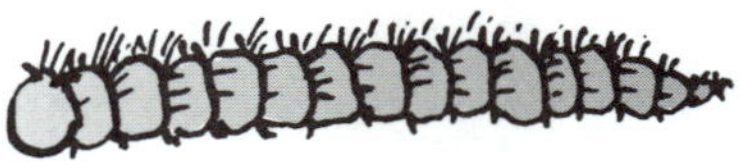

A .... B ....

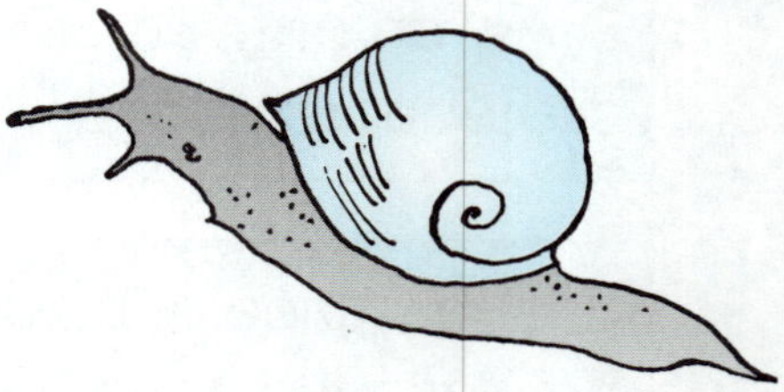

C .... D ....

LEVEL 4

MARKS

The caterpillar is part of a food chain. The picture shows the food chain.

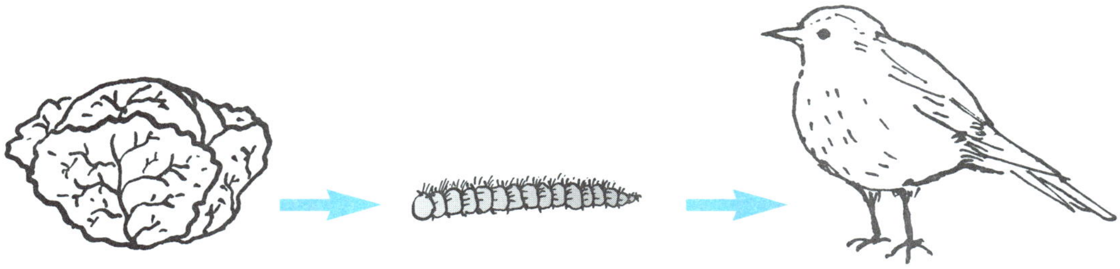

cabbage caterpillar bird

b Write down one other type of food for the caterpillar.

....

1 Q13b

c Where does the energy come from to keep the cabbage alive?

....

1 Q13c

d The caterpillar is the prey in this food chain. Write down the name of its predator.

....

1 Q13d

17 Air contains water in the form of vapour.

Simone put some Cola in a glass. She put in some ice cubes and took the drink outside in the garden, where it was sunny.

a What did she notice on the outside of the glass?

....

1 Q17a

b Where did it come from?

....

1 Q17b

c Unscramble these letters to describe what happens to water vapour when it meets something cold.

C S N E E D N O S

....

1 Q17c

You may have seen water vapour condense in some of these places.

d Put a cross ✗ through the picture of the object that you would **not** see condensation on.

1
Q17d

inside a car window
on a cold day

inside a house
on a cold day

on a cup of coffee

on a bathroom mirror

18 Look at this picture of an electric toaster. The parts are made of different materials.

4
Q18a

a Answer each question by underlining your choice from the answers given.

1 What is the flex made of?

metal **plastic and metal** **plastic**

2 What is the handle made of?

metal **plastic and metal** **plastic**

3 What is the body of the toaster made of?

metal **plastic and metal** **plastic**

4 Which part of the flex conducts electricity?

metal **plastic and metal** **plastic**

b Why is the base made of plastic? Tick ✓ **one** box.

1 Q18b

It looks attractive. ☐

It lets very little heat pass through. ☐

It melts easily. ☐

19 Merraz and Leona are having a picnic on the beach.

a Draw the Sun on the picture to show where it would have been an hour ago.

1 Q19a

b Tick ✓ the reason why the position of the Sun changes.

1 Q19b

The Sun moves round the Earth. ☐

The Earth moves round the Sun. ☐

The Earth spins round on its axis. ☐

20 Who can see the television picture?

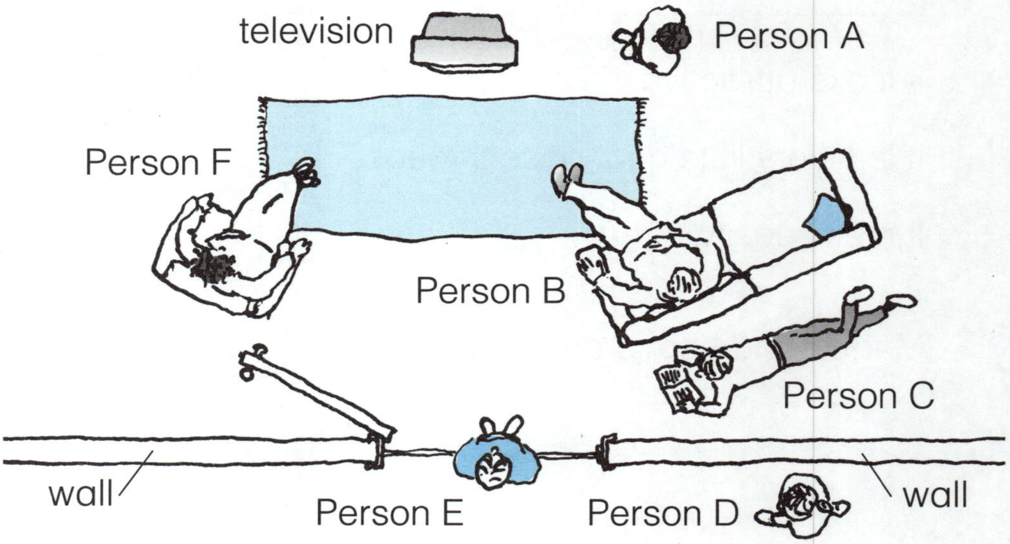

3
Q20a

a Write down the people who can see the television.

Person .... Person .... Person ....

1
Q20b

b Complete the words in the sentence to describe how light travels.

Light travels to our eyes in a s............ l............ .

1
Q20c

c Draw a line to show what happens when light from the torch hits the mirror.

d How does the mirror help the driver to see what is behind, without turning round?

....

....

1 Q20d

21 Below is a list of things that change.

Put a tick ✓ in the table to show which can be changed back and which cannot. The first one has been done for you.

	Can be changed back	Cannot be changed back
Striking a match		✓
Melting ice		
Baking a cake		
Freezing water		
Burning coal		

4 Q21

22 Jo and Terry like to camp in the winter snow.

They make a cup of tea starting with some snow.

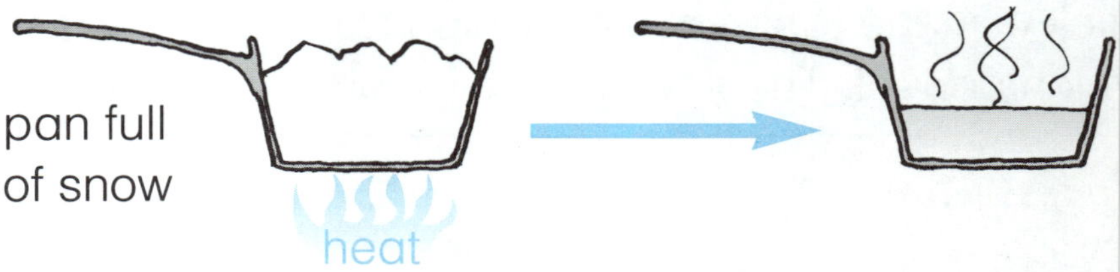

Answer the questions by putting a tick ✓ in the correct box.

2
Q22

a When the snow changes into water it:

freezes	☐
melts	☐
boils	☐

b After Jo and Terry have made the tea they put the pan of water outside in the snow. The water slowly changes into ice. The water:

condenses	☐
evaporates	☐
freezes	☐

Letts

MARKS

23 Why do we have day and night?

a Fill in the missing words in these sentences.

1 Our light comes from the ....

2 The Earth turns round once every .... hours.

3 The part of the Earth facing the Sun is in ....

4 The part of the Earth facing away from the Sun is in

....

4 Q23a

b Shade the part of the Earth where it is night.

1 Q23b

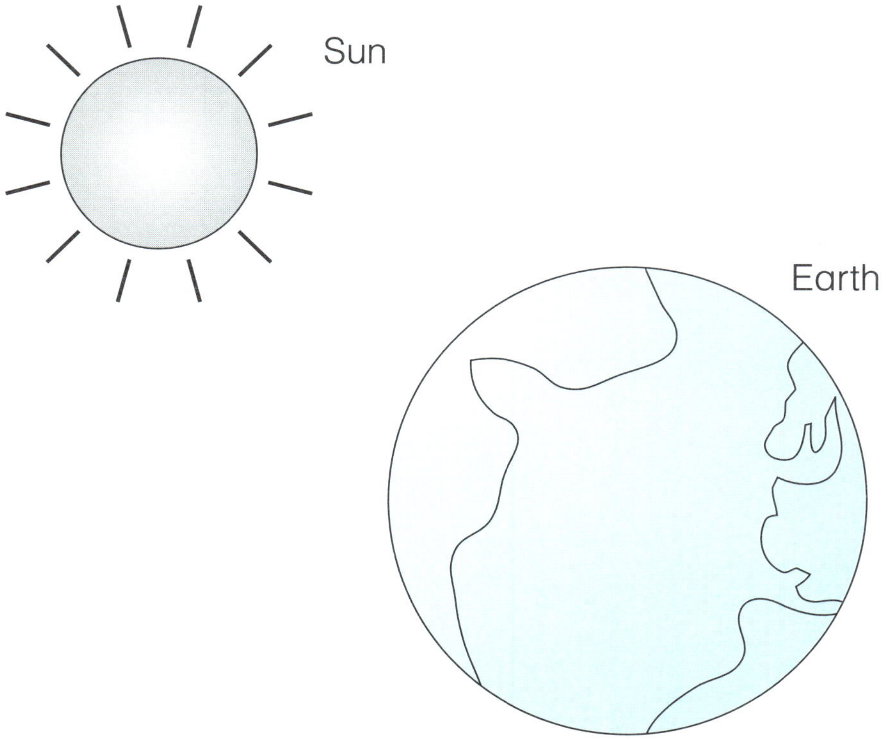

24 Leah is investigating a spring.

She hangs different weights on the end and measures how long the spring is.

Here are her results.

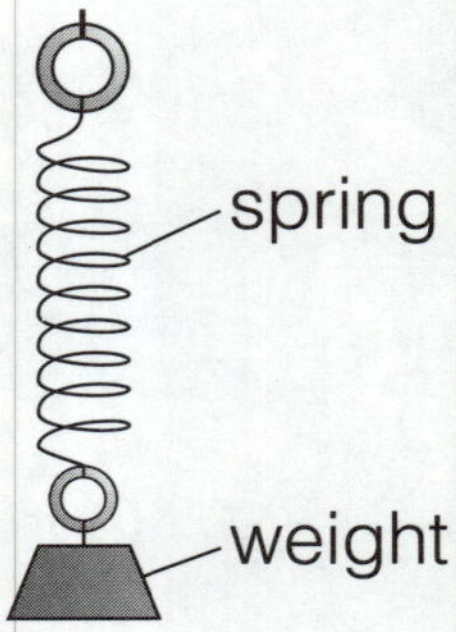

Weight on spring	Length of spring
50 grams	5.0 cm
100 grams	7.5 cm
200 grams	12.5 cm
250 grams	16.0 cm
300 grams	20.0 cm

Two of her results have been plotted on a line graph.

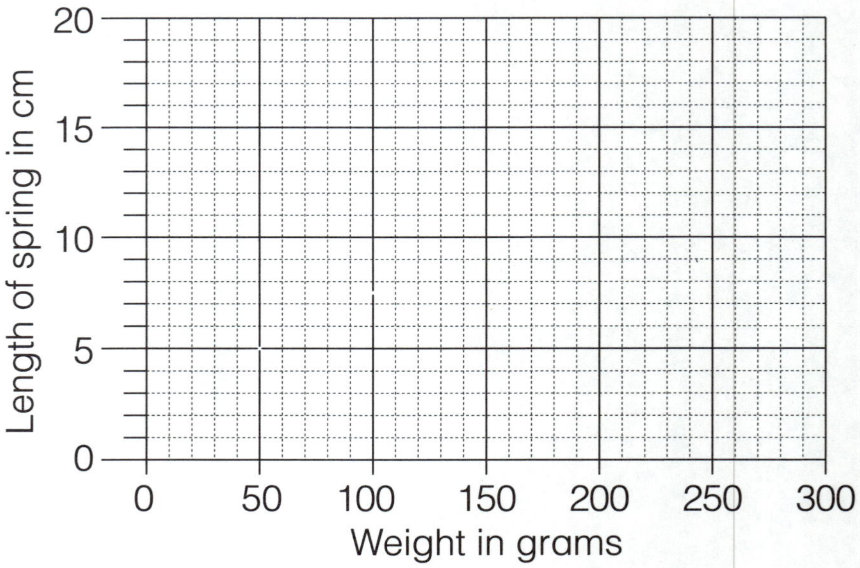

MARKS

a Finish the graph by plotting the other three points.

2 Q24a

b Draw the best line between the points.

2 Q24b

Leah forgot to write down the length of the spring when 150 grams was hung on the end.

c Use your graph to find this length.

1 Q24c

Length of spring = ... cm

d How long was the spring with no weights on the end?

1 Q24d

.... cm

Leah writes down, "The spring stretches by 5 cm for each 100 grams."

e Use the graph to find out if this is true.

2 Q24e

....

....

....

25 This picture shows the life-cycle of a plant.

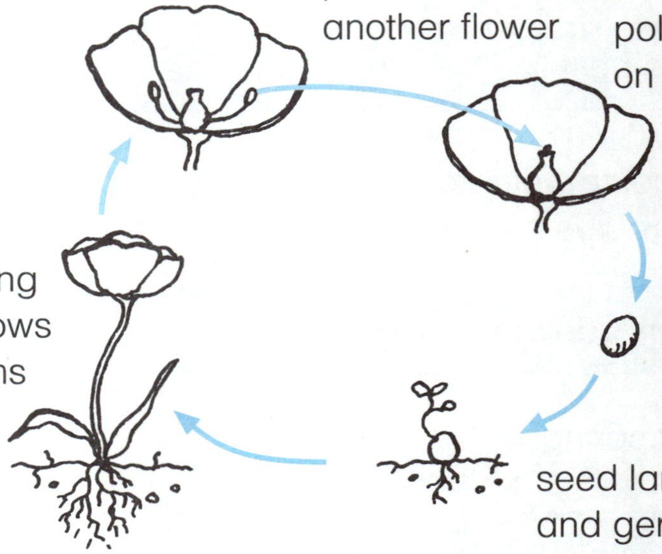

a How is pollen carried from one flower to another?

1 Q25a

....

b What is the job of the petal?

1 Q25b

....

c Which part of the plant produces pollen?

1 Q25c

....

d Write down **two** conditions needed for the seed to germinate.

2 Q25d

1 ....

2 ....

MARKS

Here are two seeds.

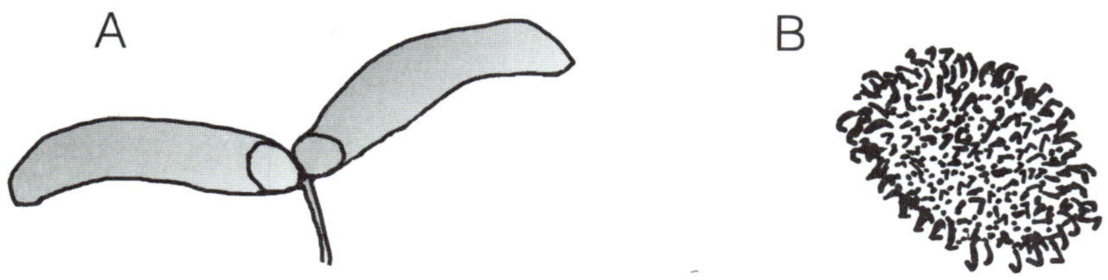

e Which seed is carried by an animal?

....

1 Q25e

f Explain how the seed is carried by an animal.

....

....

1 Q25f

26 Dissolving and filtering are two ways to separate mixtures.

a Which would you use to separate a mixture of:

flour and water? ....

flour and sugar? ....

2 Q26a

b Write down **two** reasons why a mixture of salt and sugar cannot be separated by dissolving or filtering.

1 ....

2 ....

2 Q26b

27 Inside your body you have many organs.

Some are part of your **digestive system** and are used when you eat.

Some are part of your **breathing system** and are used when you breathe in and out.

Some are part of your **circulatory system** and are used to pump blood around your body.

a Look at the list of organs below.
Put a **D** in the box if the organ is part of the digestive system.
Put a **B** if it is part of the breathing system.
Put a **C** if it is part of the circulatory system.

4 Q27a

Gullet (food pipe) ☐

Heart ☐

Lungs ☐

Stomach ☐

b What is the job of the heart?

1 Q27b

....

c What is the job of the lungs?

1 Q27c

....

d What is the job of the stomach?

1 Q27d

....

MARKS

28 The diagram shows a young baby being weighed. The weight of the baby causes a spring to stretch. This moves a pointer on the scale.

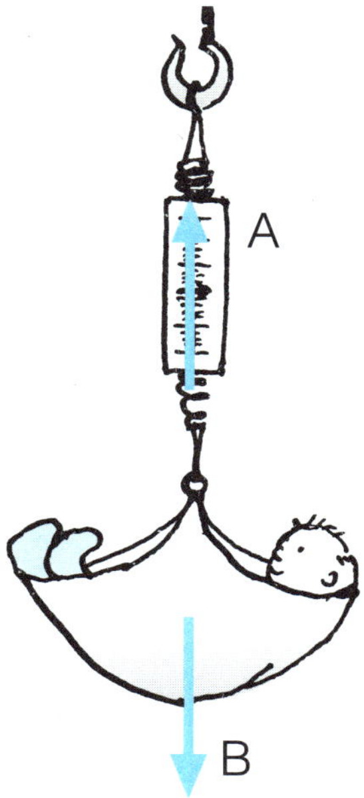

There are two forces shown on the baby.

a Use words from the list to complete the descriptions of the forces below.

4 Q28a

upward **downward** **pull** **push**

A is the .... of the spring.

B is the .... of the Earth.

The baby is held still.

b Tick ✓ the correct statement to explain why.

1 Q28b

Force A is bigger than force B. ☐

Force B is bigger than force A. ☐

Force A and force B are the same size. ☐

29 Here is a circuit that Alice made.

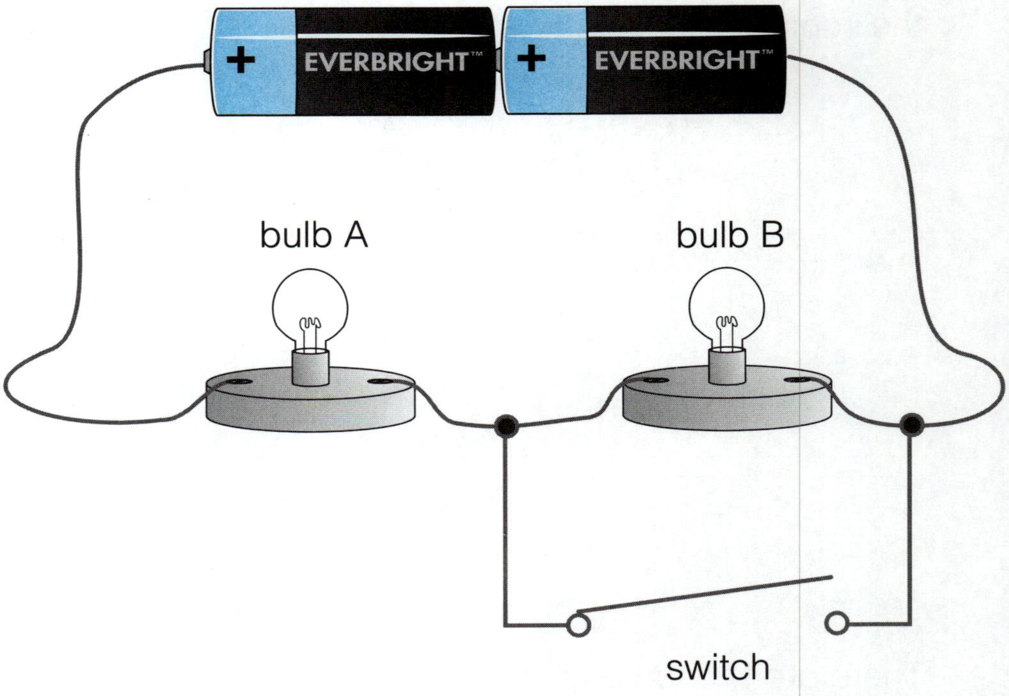

When Alice presses the switch, bulb B goes out.

a What effect does this have on the brightness of bulb A?

.... 1 Q29a

b What effect does pressing the switch have on the current in the circuit?

.... 1 Q29b

Below are three things Alice can do to change her circuit.

c Fill in the table to describe the effect of each change.

3
Q29c

Change	Effect on current	Effect on bulb A
Add another bulb between bulb A and the batteries.		
Turn one of the batteries round.		
Add another battery so there are three in a row.		

LEVEL 5

MARKS

30 There are different types of rock in the Earth.

Sedimentary rocks are made up of layers of small particles compressed together. They are the softest type of rock.

Igneous rocks are made when magma from inside the Earth cools. They often contain crystals.

Metamorphic rocks start as sedimentary rocks. They become hardened by heat and pressure.

a Here are three pictures of different rocks. Write the name of each rock type below the picture.

3
Q30a

Slate is hard and in layers.	Limestone is soft and in layers.	Granite is hard and not in layers.

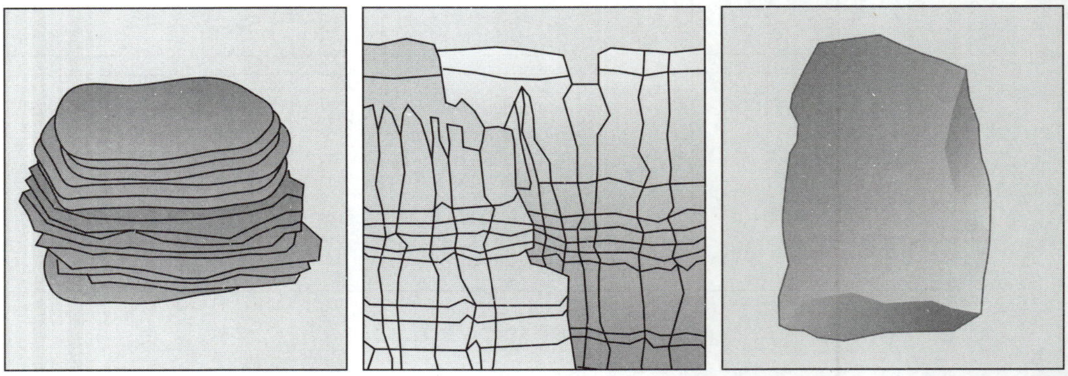

....

Letts

MARKS

b Which of the three rocks will be most easily worn away by wind and rain?

.... 1 Q30b

Slate is used for roofing.

c Write down **two** reasons why slate is a good rock for roofs.

1 ....

2 .... 2 Q30c

MARKING YOUR CHILD'S QUESTIONS

- When marking your child's questions, remember that the answers given here are the answers the question-setter expects. You must look at your child's answers and judge whether they deserve credit.
- At this age, your child's spelling may show a number of errors. Do not mark any answer wrong because the words are misspelt. Read the word aloud and, if it sounds correct, award the mark. For example, 'ekwul' would be acceptable for 'equal'.
- When you go through the questions with your child, try to be positive. Look for good things that have been done in addition to showing where errors have been made.
- Enter your child's marks on the grid on page 46, and then refer to the table below to determine your child's level.

Progress Chart

Total marks scored	Progress made	Suggested action
25 or below	Your child has acquired some of the knowledge, skills and understanding associated with work at Levels 2 and 3.	Identify areas of weakness form the Level 2 and Level 3 questions. Encourage your child to make a study of living things, to investigate the properties of everyday materials and to construct simple circuits.
26–50	Your child is confident in working with several scientific concepts at Level 3 and is beginning to show achievement at Level 4.	Encourage your child to try to explain everyday events, such as why things start or stop moving, and to be able to locate the organs of the body.
51–75	Your child has mastered Level 3 work and is showing skills associated with scientific understanding at Level 4.	Your child could use a library to investigate feeding relationships in a habitat. Encourage your child to classify everyday materials as solids, liquids or gases.
76–100	Your child is displaying the majority of the knowledge, skills and understanding required at Level 4 and is starting to grasp Level 5 ideas.	Your child could make a wall chart showing the jobs of the major organs of the body and of plants. He or she should be experimenting by using switches in electric circuits.
101 and above	Your child is making rapid progress and is already displaying aspects of Level 5 achievement.	Your child could explore separating mixtures. Techniques such as chromatography are simple to do at home. He or she should be starting to explain why organisms are found in different habitats.

- A child at the end of Year 5 (9–10 year olds) should be, of the above statements, at about the third statement.

ANSWERS

1 a two-legged animals: eagle, parrot, sparrow, child
Award two marks if all four are correct; one mark if three or two are correct — *2 marks*
four-legged animals: cat, cow, lion, goat
Award two marks if all four are corect; one mark if three or two are correct — *2 marks*
b three — *1 mark*

Note to Parent

Classification in terms of observable features is an important scientific skill which will be built on as your child progresses through Key Stages 2, 3 and 4.

Total 5 marks

2 glass – see-through — *1 mark*
iron – hard — *1 mark*
foam – soft — *1 mark*

Note to Parent

You can help your child to group materials by encouraging him or her to describe things as being hard, soft, shiny or dull.

Total 3 marks

3 It gets longer. — *1 mark*
It gets thinner. — *1 mark*

Total 2 marks

4 a Falls quickly: pound coin and plasticine — *1 mark each*
Falls slowly: feather and air-filled balloon — *1 mark each*
b screw the paper aeroplane up — *1 mark*

Total 5 marks

5 a tadpole and fish — *1 mark*
b duck and dragonfly — *1 mark*
c wings — *1 mark*

Note to Parent

The tadpole and the fish are the only ones that must stay in the water; the duck and the frog can leave. In part **c**, your child may think of feathers but this question reminds them that it is not only birds that fly.

Total 3 marks

6 sand – natural *1 mark*
cement – made *1 mark*
wood – natural *1 mark*
brick – made *1 mark*
glass – made *1 mark*
slate – natural *1 mark*
plastic – made *1 mark*

Note to Parent

A made material is one where the raw material has been processed to change it before it is used.

Total 7 marks

7 a torch *1 mark*
b personal stereo *1 mark*
c television *1 mark*

Total 3 marks

8 a

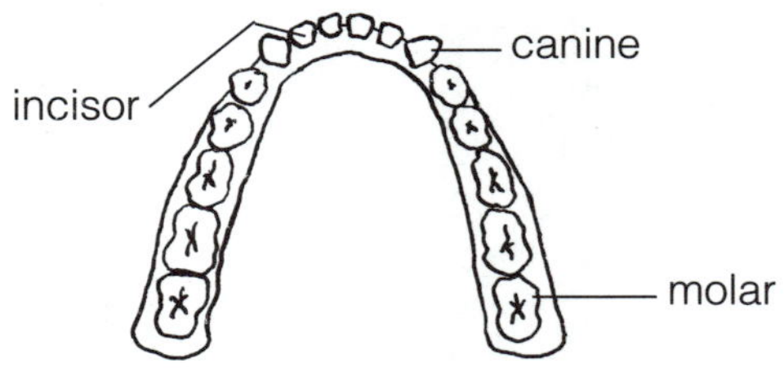

1 mark each

b 1 toothbrush, toothpaste *1 mark*
2 two, meals *1 mark*
3 dentist *1 mark*
4 decay *1 mark*

Note to Parent

This question assess whether your child appreciates the functions of different types of teeth. It also helps to reinforce the importance of dental care.

Total 7 marks

9 a it would dissolve *1 mark*
b it would evaporate *or* dry up *1 mark*
c put it in a cool place *or* add ice to it *1 mark*
d it would freeze *or* go hard *or* solidify *1 mark*
e water *or* condensation *1 mark*

Note to Parent

Encourage your child to use scientific terms, such as dissolve and evaporate, rather than 'disappears', to describe everyday events.

Total 5 marks

10 a oil and water *1 mark each*
b copper and iron *1 mark each*
c wood *1 mark*

Note to Parent

This question is assessing whether your child can sort materials according to their properties.

Total 5 marks

11 a the carpet *1 mark*
b more than *1 mark*
c C *1 mark*
d the parachute is the biggest *or* there is more air resistance *1 mark*

Total 4 marks

12 a the smoke *1 mark*
b Ben *1 mark*
c he is nearest to Eddie *1 mark*

Note to Parent

You can encourage your child to link everyday events, such as the brightness of a lamp or the loudness of a sound, to the distance from the source.

Total 3 marks

13 a Check your child has drawn the bar to a height of 8 units on the vertical scale *1 mark*
b size 2 *1 mark*
c 2 *1 mark*
d 27 *1 mark*

Note to Parent

This question is assessing your child's skill at handling data and interpreting charts. Your child should gain confidence in using bar charts and line graphs as she or he progresses through Key Stage 2.

Total 4 marks

14 a iron *or* steel *1 mark*
b opposite poles attract *1 mark*
like poles repel *1 mark*
c the boat moves to the left *1 mark*

Note to Parent

Iron and steel are the most common magnetic materials. Children enjoy playing with magnets and can be encouraged to use a magnet to sort objects, such as drinks cans.

Total 4 marks

15 a

1 mark

b friction — 1 mark

Note to Parent

Children get confused about friction forces and motion. Friction opposes sliding or slipping, and is the force that propels us forwards when we push backwards.

Total 2 marks

16 a A caterpillar — *1 mark*
B butterfly — *1 mark*
C wasp — *1 mark*
D snail — *1 mark*

Note to Parent

Your child may try to guess the name by just looking at the picture. Encourage your child to follow the key.

b Any green plant — *1 mark*
c the Sun — *1 mark*
d bird — *1 mark*

Total 7 marks

17 a water drops *or* condensation — *1 mark*
b from the air — *1 mark*
c condenses — *1 mark*
d cup of coffee — *1 mark*

Note to Parent

If your child answered 'water vapour' to part **a**, then she or he has not yet learned to distinguish between the states of water. Condensation is water in a liquid form that is formed when water vapour in the air is cooled.

Total 4 marks

18 a 1 plastic and metal — *1 mark*
2 plastic — *1 mark*
3 metal — *1 mark*
4 metal — *1 mark*
b It lets very little heat pass through. — *1 mark*

Note to Parent

Question 18 assesses whether your child is able to relate the properties of materials to their everyday uses, and knows that some materials are better thermal insulators than others and better electrical conductors than others.

Total 5 marks

19 a The Sun should be drawn higher in the sky and to the left, for example: *1 mark*

b The Earth spins round on its axis. *1 mark*

Note to Parent

This question assesses your child's knowledge of how the apparent position of the Sun changes over the course of the day, in an arc from west to east and overhead at midday. The Earth spins on its axis one complete rotation every 24 hours – this accounts for the apparent movement of the Sun in the sky and for day and night.

Total 2 marks

20 a In any order:
B E F *1 mark each*

b straight line *1 mark*

c The line should show the reflected light making the same angle with the mirror surface as the torch beam does. *1 mark*

d it reflects the light *1 mark*

Note to Parent

Your child should understand that light usually travels in straight lines and is reflected in a predictable way by mirrors and other shiny surfaces.

Total 6 marks

21 Can be changed back: melting ice and freezing water *1 mark each*
Cannot be changed back: baking a cake and burning coal *1 mark each*

Note to Parent

This question assesses your child's ability to make predicitons about whether changes are reversible or not.

Total 4 marks

22 a melts *1 mark*
b freezes *1 mark*

Total 2 marks

23 a 1 Sun *1 mark*
2 24 *1 mark*
3 daylight *1 mark*
4 darkness *1 mark*
b The half of the Earth not facing the Sun should be shaded *1 mark*

Note to Parent

Children often confuse the Earth's spin on its axis and its movement around the Sun. A model using a ball and a table lamp can help their understanding.

Total 5 marks

24 a Check your child has correctly plotted the three points

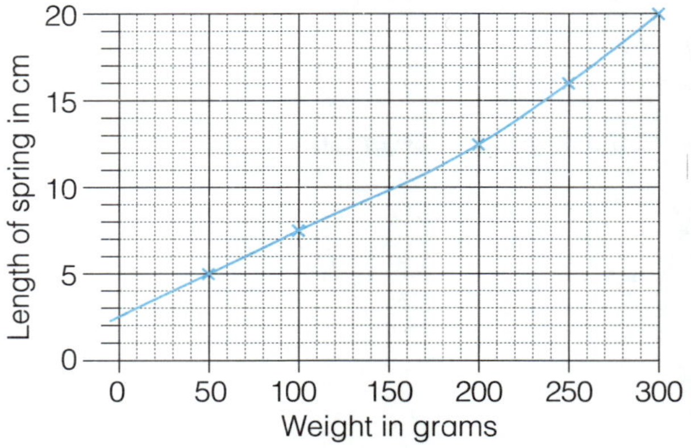

Award two marks for three correctly plotted points; one mark for two or one point *2 marks*
b A straight line should be drawn between the first three points *1 mark*
A curve should be drawn between the last three points *1 mark*

Note to Parent

Your child should be discouraged from joining the points together when drawing line graphs in science. The data from science experiments is not exact – the points on the graph merely show the trend.

c 10 cm — *1 mark*
d 2.5 cm — *1 mark*

Note to Parent

The length without any weights is found by continuing the line backwards and reading the length for a weight of 0 grams.

e It is true for the first 200 grams — *1 mark*
After that the spring stretches more than 5 cm for each 100 grams — *1 mark*

Note to Parent

At Level 4, your child should be beginning to use graphs to spot patterns and trends in experimental data.

Total 8 marks

25 a by sticking to the bodies of insects — *1 mark*
b to attract insects — *1 mark*
c the stamen *or* anther — *1 mark*

Note to Parent

A common error at this level is to confuse the stamen and the stigma. The stamen, which consists of a filament and an anther, is the male part of the flower which produces the pollen. The pollen then lands on the female stigma during pollination.

d *Any two of:*
air, moisture, warmth — *1 mark each*

Note to Parent

Many children think that a seed needs soil to germinate. The conditions needed for germination can be investigated at home using cress seeds and kitchen paper.

e B — *1 mark*
f tiny hooks become attached to the animal's fur — *1 mark*

Note to Parent

This question is testing an understanding of different ways in which seeds are adapted for dispersal.

Total 7 marks

26 a flour and water – filtering — *1 mark*
flour and sugar – dissolving — *1 mark*
b they are both solid so they cannot be filtered — *1 mark*
they both dissolve in water — *1 mark*

Note to Parent

Some children confuse the processes of sieving and filtering. Sieving is a process used to separate solid particles of different sizes. Filtering separates a solid from a liquid.

Total 4 marks

27 a	Gullet D	*1 mark*
	Heart C	*1 mark*
	Lungs B	*1 mark*
	Stomach D	*1 mark*
b	to pump blood around the body	*1 mark*
c	for breathing *or* to exchange gases	*1 mark*
d	to digest food	*1 mark*

Note to Parent

Your child should be starting to identify major organs with their corresponding organ systems, and to describe the function of major organs. The main organ systems are skeletal, respiratory, digestive, ciculatory, nervous, reproduction and urinary.

Total 7 marks

28 a	A: upward, pull	*1 mark each*
	B: downward, pull	*1 mark each*
b	Force A and force B are the same size.	*1 mark*

Note to Parent

When an object is not moving, the forces on it are balanced, so the effect of a force in one direction is cancelled out by the effect of a force in the oppostie direction.

Total 5 marks

29 a increases the brightness *1 mark*

b increases the current *1 mark*

c

Change	Effect on current	Effect on bulb A	
Add bulb	decreases	gets dimmer	*1 mark*
Turn battery	decreases *or* no current	gets dimmer *or* goes out	*1 mark*
Add battery	increases	gets brighter	*1 mark*

Note to Parent

Turning a battery round could have either effect, depending on the condition of the two batteries.

Total 5 marks

30 a slate is metamorphic *1 mark*
limestone is sedimentary *1 mark*
granite is igneous *1 mark*

Note to Parent

In this question your child is being asked to use information given in the question to classify the rocks. He or she is not expected to know the different types of rock.

b limestone *1 mark*

Note to Parent

The effects of the weather on limestone can be seen on buildings and in graveyards.

c slate is waterproof *1 mark*
it splits easily into thin layers *1 mark*

Total 6 marks

MARKING GRID

LEVEL 2 Pages 1–3

Question	Marks available	Marks scored
1	5	
2	3	
3	2	
4	5	
Total	**15**	

LEVEL 3 Pages 4–13

Question	Marks available	Marks scored
5	3	
6	7	
7	3	
8	7	
9	5	
10	5	
11	4	
12	3	
13	4	
Total	**41**	

LEVEL 4 Pages 14–27

Question	Marks available	Marks scored
14	4	
15	2	
16	7	
17	4	
18	5	
19	2	
20	6	
21	4	
22	2	
23	5	
24	8	
Total	**49**	

LEVEL 5 Pages 28–35

Question	Marks available	Marks scored
25	7	
26	4	
27	7	
28	5	
29	5	
30	6	
Total	**34**	